Tiny Bright Tho:

Jen Feroze

Published by Nine Pens Press

2024

www.ninepens.co.uk

ISBN: 978-1-917150-04-0

023

What Do You Do?

After Chrissie Dreier

I try to hold on
to small pieces of myself
amid all this love.

The Fourth Trimester

These first weeks are uncharted and you are adrift
in seas the same colour and temperature as tears.
And you are weightless with exhaustion in the water,
the scope of need making hollow driftwood of your bones,
all your past selves floating out of reach,
clumps of green, unfettered seaweed.

Slowly, you are discerning shorelines and horizons
in the dark, and slowly you are swimming.
And the waters bloom with jellyfish,
vicious moon bodies lit with guilt and doubt,
and you are firebranded, but you are swimming.
And then there are shallows, there are footholds.

There are others like you, crawling stunned and stung
onto the shingle. There is a sunrise cresting the waves,
tongues of flame in your hair. Slowly you stand.
You stand and pass the bright certainty of dawn
along this beach like a beacon,
mother to mother to mother.

When, At Bedtime, I Ask My Daughter What She Wants To Be When She Grows Up, And She Says 'A Fox'

I could have smiled
and said 'no, darling,
that's not what I meant'.
I could have proffered
doctor
    teacher
        plumber
            painter.

Instead, I turn out the lights.
Instead, I draw down stars and pines.
Instead we sharpen our teeth and lengthen our tails,
we drink up the moonlight.

And we careen around her bedroom,
leaving pawmarks like poems or prayers in a carpet of snow.

Don't Buy Her Flowers

For there is already too much
fragility between these walls
and it terrifies her.
She is learning to swim
in the moonlight and soft fog of these rooms,
made unfamiliar with sleeplessness
and the feathered cries of the new.

She is building palaces
from sofa cushions, rebuilding
herself from buttered crusts and cold tea.
She is exploring the curious pain
of her heart expanding, her rib cage
more a cathedral of feeling
than she ever thought possible.

Don't buy her flowers.
For as time stretches like treacle
she will be powerless to do anything
but watch them die. As life contracts
to the tiny curves and hollows of his face,
his warm body, they will scatter pollen
into the hearth like golden soot,
their petals leached of colour –
papyrus with nothing to say.

Instead, show her the village of lanterns
you've left blazing in your windows.
Bring her star-crusted nights

as a balm to her itching eyes. Let her feel
the comforting weight and substance
of all your little anchors,
neighbouring boats rocked by the same deep tide.

The Weather App Gives A 100% Chance Of Snow

And I am warmed
by the thought of all that cold.
The world will be made new
again, even if just for a few hours.
My daughter can leave fresh footprints in something,
can play a monochromatic version of I Spy
in these same old streets
where everything suddenly begins with 's'.
My fingers thrill with future chilblains,
with the idea of trailing runes
into the softness of the neighbour's garden wall.

I leave the blind half open when I go to bed,
to give us the chance of catching
those first, fat flakes. Wanting to hold
my baby son up to the window
marble-eyed with this wide night
and say 'look. Look how the sky falling
doesn't always mean disaster.' Then 4am
and the snow is a sloppy drunk,
barely more than rain, lurching
across the streetlight's glow in messy gusts.
My baby son stays in his crib. I pull the duvet higher.

When the sun eventually drags itself out of bed,
apologies from the clouds streak the windowpanes.
Nothing has changed.

Maternal Zoology

Lights out on the post-labour ward,
hot as the tropics, and sound fills the room.
Each of us sits heavy in our cubicles,
air stagnant with sweat and milk,
blood's iron tang and a herbaceous bite
of exquisite and terrifying love.

Amid the beeps, the buzzers
and the hum of fluttering midwives,
vines are growing around our curtained walls.

Across from me, there's a mangrove swamp,
silted and warmly green,
filled with the clicking and squeaking
of bright midnight frogs.
Two cubicles over is lush
with sudden, sodden jungle;
a tenderness of soft primate hoots.

Our own little landscape is a miniature aviary,
your tiny lips curving into twitters
and snatches of pitchy song.
I croon along with you until your breathing
slows into sleep;
stroking your back, imagining
the beginnings of wings.

Next door,
wavelets of quiet sobbing
lap against the edge of the bed.

As the night deepens,
I want to reach into the water –
a glowing, hospital blue –
and help keep her afloat.

Upon Being Faced With The Penguin Book of Baby Names

First, allow its pages to fall open
seemingly at random.
Treat its bookshop-fresh smell with reverence,
as if it's the I Ching, or perhaps
a silk pouch of stones, river-smooth
and carved with ancient runes.
Flick and stop. Flick and stop.
Sweep the text with your eyes,
searching for a hook to hang a personality upon.

Be systematic
in your quest for meaning.
Circle names that signal kindness, strength, loyalty,
the ability to cook a proper roast dinner,
to remember important birthdays and celebrations,
to seek peace among trees and on shorelines,
the ability to find love and hold it close, to know
when to ask for help and where to find it,
to be sincere and steadfastly alright.

Comb your combined histories
for associations with bullies at primary school –
that guy you worked with who chewed
with his mouth open; the girl whose laugh
was part wading bird, part cheese grater.
Speak names out loud and wait for a sign
from within, an elbow to the underside of your ribs
that says: '*closer. Closer. Yes.*
This is who I am.'

Then, when sleep inevitably eludes you,
think of the blue plaque you found in north London:
'Namer of Clouds lived and died here'.
Think of those who christen colours, so we can paint our walls
in dawn skies, sugared lilac, elephant's breath.

Imagine candlelit rooms
speckled with earnest lexicographers,
centuries ago, pinning meanings down on paper
like butterflies.

When, At Bedtime, I Ask My Daughter If She's OK. And She Says, 'Yes Mummy. Are You?'

I could have smiled
and said 'yes, darling,
don't worry I'm just a bit tired'.
I could have lit the wicks
behind
      each
           exhausted
                  eye.

Instead I turn out the lights.
Instead, I sit mute on her bedroom floor.
Instead I let her small hands trace heart shapes
and magic spells on my back.

And eventually she gives in to sleep,
launching dreams at the ceiling like dauntless porcelain birds.

The Night The Whales Came

After Lucy Campbell's 'They Sing To Remember Us'

She had been thinking of flight,
damp rising like a wound
on the holdall in the base of the boat.
The mouth of the river yawned
a few prowlengths ahead, and stillness
dripped thickly from her oars like mercury.

Then she looked up and there they were,
bellies grooved with stars,
swimming lazily in the sky, hypnotic in their vastness.
Their fins were cumulus, seamed with traces of light,
and though she couldn't hear them,
she knew that they were singing.

She sat and watched them for a while,
their unlikely grace, their serenity,
their coaxing of dawn from horizon's darkest places –
hulking celestial midwives.

She stayed until dewpoint,
until droplets of day glittered her sleeves,
and the mound of her stomach,
until they encircled her neck
like tight little futurepearls. Then she turned
and rowed back towards the lights of home.

For My Son On Valentines Day

I do love nothing in the world so well as you, is that not strange?
– William Shakespeare

I don't yet know the way your laugh sounds,
fully fledged. Whether it gurgles up like a stream,
snickers in whispers behind furtive palms, or bursts forth
in an unstoppable blast of mirth.
I don't know what you dream about,
the dozens of ways you'll leave your mark. I don't know
the places you'll go, whether you'll seek
hot crowds or silent sunrise.
I don't know your ultimate hangover breakfast,
the way your arms feel flung around my neck,
the way the planes of your face look
with 5' o clock shadow, the way the planes of your face look
when not cushioned in the chubby velvet of infancy.
Whether or not you can roll your 'r's,
roll your tongue, roll a cigarette.
Whether your hands are as big as your father's,
able to hold my face like it's the sun.

Some of these I may never know –
locks with keys held by other loves.
All I do know is the way you need me.
All I do know is that five months ago today
you were lifted bloody and mewling onto my chest,
and you brought with you a gush of love
so ferociously pure it's a wonder
it didn't burn that clean white room to the ground.

Maternal Audiology

How would you rate your mood on a scale of 1 to 5?

5	4	3	2	1
[Christmas euphoria]				[the pull of the riptide]

Do you have adequate support systems around you?

5	4	3	2	1
[A bosomy stage dive]				[flaccid celery in the fridge]

Have you ever mistaken anything for the sound of your child crying?
[use blank sheet provided]

All water that moves –
showersinkwashingmachinedish-
washerrivertaptide
the old oak shaking   itself free of leaves

a squirrel's chuntering bark
shrieking blue lights   echoes of the playground

two streets away, the drilling   from the house
with the green door nesting pigeons in the   eaves.

My own voice.   The thick
incredulity of silence.

Mum appears fine, calm and rational. Baby is healthy.

Duality

Firing off a message to a friend –
'I'll have to call you back

once the kids are in bed', I am again
staggered by adulthood, its certainty

sharp as a backhand to the cheek,
black as mortgage statement ink.

Lately the mirrors seem to ripple with history,
I see shades of myself as a child,

as *my* child, as my mother. I pluck silver
from my scalp with a magpie's curiosity,

still occasionally clockwatch, waiting
for the professional grown-ups to arrive.

I'd like to try and stop the pendulum swing,
to swing instead for acceptance of age for what it is:

to be at once mother and child, the soil and the stardust,
the rush and the riverbed.

Self Portrait At 35 Weeks

Not the moon,
but her reflection caught in a pond.
My tenderly planted bed, latticed by slugs –
a seemingly overnight silvering
of this pungent earth.
Something you'd find glazed
on the bottom shelf of a bakery. A bag
thrashing with fairground fish.
An upturned bowl of porridge.
Oh, you slow-punctured water bed.
Oh! You magnetic globe for strangers' hands,
the unwelcome and the minuscule, pushing
as if against a curved pane of glass.

A Sunday In March

The Earth has, incredibly, sent itself
halfway around the Sun,
and you are beating your fists
on the hallway mirror enthralled,
agape at the wonder of your own face.

Sweetheart, there's never been anyone like you.

In these sluggish, elastic months since your birth,
there hasn't been anyone even close.
You've never seen another baby.
We row row row our boat down gentle streams alone,
while far-flung grandparents coo through screens
and I try not to feel adrift when packing away
an ascending scale of tiny clothes.
There will be so many stories told
of the cavernous strangeness into which you were born,
just you wait. One day we will run
to meet the summer, and our garden, our doorway,
our kitchen chairs will sprout with a warmth of people.
You'll be amazed by new voices,
new laps, new embraces.
Your chubby hand will grasp and catch
something other than its own reflection.

A Duplex For Rumpelstiltskin

He should have known better,
the jewels came so easily from her neck.

So easily, or so he thought. Simple jewels, barely shining
but set in gold, coaxed into his clawed hands.

She watched his twisted hands coaxing gold from straw,
hay-scent becoming riches recognised by men, by kings.

She was straw-scented as king's riches swelled within her
and she remembered everything she'd ever heard.

Everything she'd ever heard whispered in the woods noted,
logged like the sacks of flour in the old barn.

She is heavy as a sack of flour, dulled and heavy, he thinks.
Slowly she lulled him as he spun.

Now she is a mother, spinning slowly among her baby's playthings.
She knows all their names. He should have known better.

Maternal Horology
After Salvador Dali

What does it say, then,
that I make sense of these drooling clocks?
Here the greasy string
cheese of minutes spent cajoling over socks
and shoes, there
a pocket watch flung like wet laundry
in a two-year-old storm over the blasted stump
of my patience. The ants are mocking me with
their ticking feet. *Late, again.*
Late.

The Midtown museum on 53rd street,
points out the 'monstrous fleshy creature
draped across the painting'. How alien it is!
the experts shout. How disturbing! I see
myself and others like me. We
the ragged frazzle of exhaustion.
We the melting custodians
of these tar-thick early days.

I'll take the next shift.
Get some sleep.
Keep your eyes
on that golden horizon.

This, too, shall pass.

Reunion

After Claudine Toutoungi

This should be easy as breathing –
after all, we used to build worlds
out of conversations. Spin debates
into spiral staircases, or glassy bars
where we'd charm the bartenders and the men
and the spirits from the trees. We've been known
to conjure fireworks above spires in the rain;
the whole sprawl of Paris
from your grubby sofa.

I compliment your hair.
You say thank you.
We both stare
with something
like bemusement
at my children.

When, At Bedtime, I Think My Daughter Is Asleep
And She Mutters 'Mummy, Your Face Is A Raindrop'

I could have smiled
and climbed into a soft slice
of bed next to her.
I could have forgotten the
indignant

      screaming
           at
                dinner.

Instead, I creep backwards out of the room.
Instead I drink wine with my husband.
Instead I turn my old raindrop face to the TV,
dishes left in the sink.

And I leave her to her stormy sleep,
hair a gathering cumulus over the pillow.

Dinner For One

This is a different kind of happiness,
sitting like a gentle curiosity
in the corner of the pub, miles from home.
I eat slowly: pink flakes of salmon,
baby potatoes, artichoke hearts
dripping oil; fork balanced in one hand,
head down and reading.

I finish when I'm bored of the taste,
order dessert despite not clearing my plate.
Tonight I am nobody's role model.

The route back to the stranger's house –
neatly made bed, small talk in the kitchen –
is edged with a clean fear of the dark
pushing against my circle of torch.
I've spent too long in the well-lit town,
am out of practice with walking in the middle
of a blackened road, the embrace of trees
and a cold jolt of stars overhead.

An Extrapolation of Magpies

They say eight's a wish, nine's a kiss. What then,
am I to do with this? This chatterclack,
this featherstatic, this black and white
noise in the tree outside your window?

Eleven's an impatience.

Nonetheless, it is nap time.
We've bounced and we've jiggled.
You've giggled and pointed and
yelled and kicked and danced and (once) bitten.

Twelve's a clenched jaw

Now you're cotton soft, slightly bobbled, limbs
encased in hand-me-down love,
milk beading on your lips. The baby
from the magazine again.

Thirteen is faint surprise at the readiness of tears.

Nearly there, heavy lids,
my waterfall of sibilant gibberish,
aping the hush of distant waves. Aching
to put you down. Aching to draw you back inside me.

Fourteen's a simple   r e n d i n g   of a self.

There are things I should be doing.

Fifteen's a dishwasher full of knives, blade up.

There are things I should be doing.

Sixteen's a vow stretched taut.

Look out at this tree of omens
and wait for my cue;
a sound like applause.

There are things I should be doing.

Stained Glass

Preparing for your arrival, I take apart pieces of myself,
packing my old life, several of my dreams,
my selfishness, carefully away
like panels of stained glass before a rain of bombs.
I bury them under the river of my blood, in the crypt,
a hiding place where I can sometimes pore over them,
remembering the pictures they once made.

Your birth was the explosion,
the blood and the fire. You made me
a smoking pile of sleepless rubble and milk
and shaken memories. And I'd never felt more beautiful.
I claimed my new title with hungry hands,
tried not to flinch at the sparks of colour
that flashed in my body's vaults;
that lodged in my heart like tiny bright thorns
with every deep breath.

One day, we will dig up that old glass together.
Some shards will be broken,
others missing, buried too deep.
And you will show me how to make new pictures.
Your small hands surprisingly tender, careful
with the fragments, holding them up to the light
and shocking us both with their rainbows.

When The World Ends

I will think about the blue whale skeleton
in the Natural History Museum
after the doors are closed.
The way its inverted hull of ribs floats
lazily and alone amid the darkened arches,
mosaics and tourist information desks.
I will remember that some earnest optimist
christened it Hope. I will wonder
if it carries deep, shuddering songs in its old bones.

I will think about ghost apples
in twinkling Michigan orchards.
Their flesh and juice slurried to the ground.
Everything that makes them apples
decayed under a crust of snow,
and empty, frozen baubles left suspended
like gifts from Grimm.

I will think about the names of moths
and taste them very deliberately with my mind.
Currant Clearwing. Feathered Gothic.
Liquorice Piercer. Burnet Companion

And while I am thinking, I will hold you.
Will contort my body to make us a family
of matryoshka dolls, nested close.
I will think about all these places that hold magic,
and I will bite my tongue.

You see, were I to open my mouth,
you would see the sun burning inside,
and the wildfire of *I love you*
would crackle up and out.

There wouldn't be space left to breathe.

Acknowledgments

Thanks are due to the editors of *Blood Moon Journal, The Mum Poem Press, Chestnut Review, Gingernut Magazine, Ink Sweat & Tears, Dust, Poetry Wales and Train River Publishing* where some of these poems first appeared.

9 781917 150040